# DELICIOUS EMPANADA RECIPES

## World's Most Famous Empanadas

Danny Gansneder

ISBN-13: 978-1517144951

ISBN-10: 1517144957

# CONTENTS

# CONVERSION TABLE

- 1/ 2 fl oz = 3 tsp = 1 tbsp = 15 ml

- 1 fl oz = 2 tbsp = 1/ 8 c = 30 ml

- 2 fl oz = 4 tbsp = 3/ 4 c = 60 ml

- 4 fl oz = 8 tbsp = 1/ 2 c = 118 ml

- 8 fl oz = 16 tbsp = 1 c = 236 ml

- 16 fl oz = 1 pt = 1/ 2 qt = 2 c = 473 ml

- 128 fl oz = 8 pt = 4 qt = 1 gal = 3.78 L

# ABBREVIATIONS

- oz = ounce

- fl oz = fluid ounce

- tsp = teaspoon

- tbsp = tablespoon

- ml = milliliter

- c = cup

- pt = pint

- qt = quart

- gal = gallon

- L = liter

# INTRODUCTION

An Empanada is a small meat pie made from meat cheese, or fish with either a vegetable or fruit filling.

There is no stipulated time when Empanadas are to be eaten; you can have them at any time of the day, at breakfast, lunch or even supper. Since most Empanadas are made from sweat fillings, they are very good for desert.

Empanadas can be stuffed with many different kinds of fillings, from sugary filing to savory filling. The best part about preparing empanadas is that you can also come up with your own filling and create something amazing.

## EMPANADA DOUGH

This flaky outer layer is the basic crust and is perfect for making Empanadas. Just add your favorite filling to the dough and cook.

- 3 cups flour
- 2 teaspoons sugar
- Pinch of salt
- 1/2 cup shortening
- 3 teaspoons baking powder
- 3/4 cup chicken stock
- 1 egg

- Oil for frying

Mixing all the dry ingredients beat the egg into the mixture and then add the chicken broth. Blend the egg and the broth to form dough. After the dough is formed take the mixture and put it in the refrigerator for half an hour.

Roll out the dough on a floured table to about 1/8 inches. Then cut off small circles that will be used for the Empanadas. When you are done cut out the circles fold them in half and seal them using a fork, then cook following the recipe

## SWEET EMPANADA DOUGH RECIPE

- 3 cups all-purpose flour

- 1/2 cup sugar

- Pinch of salt

- 2 sticks butter, cut into 16 pieces

- 2 eggs

- 2-4 tablespoons of cold water

Add together flour, sugar and salt in a bowl and mix them together in a processor.

Continue adding butter, eggs and water in the mixture until when a dough forms. After the dough is formed remove it and knead it for a while to make sure it is thick enough. Then cover it and place it in the fridge for half an hour.

Roll out the dough on a flat surface to a thickness of about 1/8 inches, cut circles and fill them with whatever dessert you want or sweet filling you want and bake them.

## CHOCOLATE EMPANADA DOUGH RECIPE

- 3 cups all-purpose flour

- 3/4 cup cocoa powder, unsweetened

- 1/2 cup sugar

- Pinch of salt

- 1 teaspoon cinnamon powder

- 2 sticks of unsalted butter, cut into small pieces

- 2 eggs

- 4-6 tablespoons of water

Mix together the flour, sugar, cocoa powder, cinnamon powder and salt into a food processor. After the mixture is well stirred add the butter make sure it well mixed. After that beat the eggs into the mixture followed by water and mix until a dough is formed.

When the dough is formed knead it a little bit and put it in the fridge for half an hour. Roll it on a flat surface to make 1/8 inch dough and cut small circles. Then fill the cut circles with any dessert you want or sweet fillings that you desire.

## SWEET PINEAPPLE EMPANADAS

- 1 cup butter, softened

- 2 pkgs cream cheese, softened

- 2 cups all-purpose flour

- 1 cup pineapple tropical fruit jam

- 1/3 cup sugar

- 1 teaspoon ground cinnamon

Into a large bowl add butter and cream cheese, followed by flour mixing until a dough is formed. Form a ball and wait for about an hour to let it chill.

While waiting preheat the oven to 375 degrees, grease a cookie sheet. Roll out the dough to about 1/8 inch thickness and cut it into circles.

Pour 1 teaspoon of jam in the middle of each circle. Sprinkle a bit of water on the edge of the dough and fold it into a half and seal it.

After that place the Empanadas on the cookie sheet that you had greased earlier and bake it in the oven for 12 minutes. Take another bowl and mix sugar cinnamon, and then sprinkle the mixture on top of the Empanadas when ready.

## SWEET CARAMEL PIE EMPANADAS

- 8 ounces of cream cheese, softened

- 2 1/2 cups all-purpose flour

- 1 cup unsalted butter, softened

- 1/2 teaspoon sea salt

- 1/2 cup caramel sauce

- 1 tablespoon cinnamon

- 1 tablespoon sugar

- 1 egg lightly beaten with 1 teaspoon water

You start by preheating the oven to 375 degrees and greasing a baking pan. In a large bowl mix the cream cheese and butter and stir well in blender. Add flour and salt to the mixture and when a dough forms roll it out on flat surface and knead it for a minute. Then wrap the dough in a plastic wrapper and put in the fridge for 20 minutes.

Make sure that the rolled dough is 1/8 inch thick. Then cut out circles and with a spoon pour out the caramel sauce at the middle of each dough circle, fold them and seal off the edges.

Place the circular dough on the baking sheet and with brush whip on some egg wash. In a separate bowl mix sugar and cinnamon and sprinkle on top of the circular shaped dough and bake them in the oven for 15 minutes.

## COCONUT AND RICE PUDDING EMPANADAS

- 1 cup long-grain white rice

- 2 cups water

- 1 large cinnamon stick

- 1 pinch salt

- 1 can evaporated milk

- 3/4 cup condensed milk

- 1/3 cup raisins

- 1 teaspoon vanilla

- 1/2 cup sweetened coconut, shredded

- 1 egg, beaten

- 15 medium dough circles

In a cooking pot boil water and add rice, cinnamon stick and salt until it cooked and all water is absorbed. Then add milk and let it continue cooking for another 5 minutes. Then add the raisins and let it cook for another 2 minutes, after that, remove the pot from the stove and let it cool.

Preheat the oven to about 450 degrees, while greasing a baking sheet. Pour out 1 and ½ tablespoon of the cooked rice and in another tablespoon have the coconut in the middle of the dough and brush the edge with the egg wash and use the folk to seal the empanadas.

Place the empanadas on the baking sheet and let them cook in the oven for 15 minutes.

## CHOCOLATEY COCONUT EMPANADA

- 1/2 cup unsalted butter, softened

- 3 oz cream cheese, softened

- 1 1/2 cups powdered sugar

- 1/3 cup unsweetened cocoa

- 1/2 teaspoon ground cinnamon

- 1/4 teaspoon salt

- 1/4 teaspoon ground chili pepper

- 1 egg

- 1 3/4 cups all-purpose flour

- 1 cup bittersweet chocolate baking chips

- 1/4 cup sweetened flaked coconut

- Water

- 1 teaspoon shortening

- Sweetened flaked coconut, toasted

Mix together butter and cream cheese in a large bowl, then add powdered sugar, unsweetened cocoa, cinnamon, salt and lastly chili pepper. Blend it until the mixture is nicely mixed. Then add the egg and add the flour, cover the mixture and wait for a while. Then in another bowl add ½ cup of bittersweet chocolate baking chip and the coconut.

Before roll the dough of a flat surface to a 1/8 thickness, preheat the oven to 375 degrees. Make the dough into small circles and using a spoon fill the middle of the dough with fillings. Brush the edge of each circle with water and fold each of them. Place the Empanadas on the baking sheet and bake them in the oven for 8 minutes.

In another bowl melt ½ cup of bittersweet chocolate baking chips and the shortening. Sprinkle the chocolate mixture and toasted coconut over the circular Empanadas and wait until the chocolate sets.

Peachy Pie Empanadas

- 8 cups peeled and diced peaches

- 1 cup sugar

- 1/4 to 1/2 cup water

- 2 cinnamon sticks

- 3 whole cloves

- 1/4 cup cinnamon sugar mixture

- 15 medium dough circles

Skin and chop the peaches and put them in a saucepan. Add sugar, water, cinnamon and clove; boil the mixture until the peaches are tender and soft.

Pour out the excess water and throw away the cinnamon and the cloves. Pound the soft peaches and cook them again for 15 minutes, stirring them to prevent them from burning. After the 15 minutes are over remove them from the stove and set them aside.

You then preheat the oven to 350 degrees and then using a brush whip on the egg white and sprinkle cinnamon and the sugar mixture. Then put them in the oven and let them cook for 20 minutes.

## CHOCOLATE CARAMEL EMPANADAS

- 3 cups all-purpose flour

- 3/4 cup unsweetened cocoa powder

- 1/2 cup sugar

- Pinch of salt

- 1 teaspoon cinnamon powder

- 2 sticks of unsalted butter, cut into small pieces

- 2 eggs

- 4-6 tablespoons of water

- 2 16 oz jars of caramel

- Dash of salt

- 1 egg, beaten with 1 tablespoon water for egg wash

- 1/4 cup sugar

In a large bowl add flour, sugar cocoa powder, cinnamon powder and salt. Use a blender and make sure that contents of the bowl are well mixed. Add in the butter pieces and pulse and blend some more. Then add the eggs and the 4 table spoons of water and stir until a dough forms.

When the dough is formed, make 2 balls with it and flatten them and wait for half an hour. Then roll the two balls on a thin sheet and cut small circles to form empanadas.

In the middle if each circle put a spoonful of fillings, and fold each circle to seal in the fillings. With a brush swap through the top with egg wash and sprinkle a little sugar as well. Leave the empanadas for 30 or so minutes before putting them in the oven.

Before baking make sure that the oven is preheated to 375 degrees and bake them for 20 minutes.

Pumpkin and Cinnamon Empanadas

18 medium Empanada pastries

For Pumpkin Filling:

- 2 lb pumpkin, seeds and membranes removed

- 1 lb panela, broken into chunks

- 5 cloves

- 5 cinnamon sticks

- 3 cups water

- 3 all spice peppers

- 1 beaten egg

- 3 tablespoons of sugar

Chop up the pumpkin into small dices and then place a chunk of panela, add water and spices in a large bowl. Cook the pumpkins until the little pieces have all dissolved. Make the panela mixture is boiled before adding in what is left of the pumpkins and together let them boil for another 30 minutes.

Let the mixture simmer for about an hour and remove it from the stove when it starts to thicken. Let it cool for a while so that you can remove the skins from the pumpkins in order to use the pulp for the empanadas.

Using a table spoon put a spoonful of the mixture on the pastry, then fold and seal it together.

The oven should be preheated to 375 degrees. Use the egg wash and brush it on top of the Empanadas. Sprinkle some sugar on top and let them bake for 20 minutes. You can serve them warm or cold with ice cream.

## CHEESY MUSHROOM EMPANADAS

- 15 medium size dough circles

- 2 tablespoons butter

- 3 cups sliced mushrooms

- 2 cups sliced shallots

- 1/4 cup raisins

- 2 teaspoons balsamic vinegar

- 1 cup grated fontina cheese

- 1 egg, separated and lightly beaten

Melt the butter in a small pan, then add in the mushrooms, shallots and let them cook for 15 minutes. After which, you will add the raisins and balsamic and let it cook for another 3 minutes. After this remove the mixture and let it cool.

With a spoon place a spoonful of the mixture and cheese in the middle of each dough circle. Use egg white for the edges and finally fold and seal the Empanada.

After that brush the tops with egg yolk and wait for 30 minutes for it to sink in, prepare the oven by preheating it to 400 degrees. Bake it for 20 minutes and serve while hot.

## GOAT CHEESE AND ASPARAGUS EMPANADAS

- 2 tablespoons butter

- 1/2 cup finely diced white onion

- 1/2 lb of asparagus, washed and cut into 1-inch pieces

- 1 cup of fresh shelled green peas

- 1 cup of twice peeled fava beans

- 4 ounces of goat cheese, crumbled

- 1 tablespoon fresh chopped thyme

- Salt and pepper to taste

- 12-15 small dough circles

- 1 egg, beaten for egg wash

Melt butter in a pan, then add cut onions and cook them for 5 minutes. Next to be added is the asparagus which you will let cook for another five minutes. The fava beans follow then again let it cook for 3 minutes. The peas are added after the beans and the mixture let to cook for another 5 minutes, before adding the salt and pepper for favor. Remove the mixture and let it cool and when that's done through in the vegetables along with the goat cheese and the fresh thyme.

On the dough circles put a spoonful of the mixture, use water in the edges to help it seal properly. Fold the dough and seal after brushing the water on. Also brush the top with egg wash. The oven should preheated to 400 degrees before putting in the Empanadas, let them bake for 20 minutes.

MOZZARELLA CHEESE EMPANADAS

- 15 medium size dough circles

- 3 cups grated mozzarella

- 1/2 white onion, chopped finely

- 1 egg, separated and lightly beaten

- 3 tablespoons sugar

Mix together the chopped onions and the cheese. Using a spoon put the mixture on top of each dough circle. On the edges use egg white and fold and seal the dough circles. Finally brush a little amount of egg yolk on the dough circles.

Again sprinkle the top with sugar, before putting them in a preheated oven to 400 degrees for about 20 minutes.

## TURKEY AND GRAVY EMPANADAS

- 15 medium dough circles

- 2 tablespoons butter

- 1/2 white onion, sliced thinly

- 1/2 bell pepper, sliced thinly

- 4 garlic cloves, crushed

- 2 tomatoes, diced

- 1 teaspoon ground cumin

- 2 cups shredded turkey

- 2 tablespoons turkey gravy

- 2 tablespoons balsamic vinegar

- 1/2 tablespoon fresh oregano

- Salt to taste

- 1 egg, separated

Melt the butter in a pan and add onions, tomatoes, bell pepper, garlic and cumin. Let the mixture cook for 10 minutes while at the same time stirring. The shredded turkey is next into the mixture together with the blend of the turkey gravy and balsamic vinegar and let it cook for another 5 minutes. Remove the mixture and add the chopped oregano when it cools.

Using a spoon place the mixture in the center of each dough. Use the egg white on the edges and fold and seal the edges.

Finally, brush the top with the egg yolk, before placing it in a preheated oven at 400 degrees and bake for 23 minutes.

## TINY BEEF PIE EMPANADA

- 2 lb ground beef

- 1 teaspoon oil

- 1 onion, peeled and chopped

- 1/4 cup green olives, chopped

- 5 cloves of garlic, peeled and chopped

- 2 small potatoes, boiled and diced

- 2 hard boiled eggs, chopped

- 1 cup beef broth

- 1/2 cup raisins, soaked in warm water for 1 hour

Fly the onions and the garlic over medium heat for about a minute. Add the ground beef and cook till they turn brown. Then add green olives, raisins and simmer.

Cook till all the water reduces and is almost gone. Fold in the eggs and potatoes. Using a spoon fill each center of the circle and fold the dough and seal off the edges. Place the dough on the baking pan in put in the oven for 20 minutes.

## POTATO AND SAUSAGE EMPANADAS

- 3/4 cup finely chopped Spanish sausage

- 2 tablespoon olive oil

- 2 cups onions, finely chopped

- 3 garlic cloves, finely chopped

- 1 red bell pepper, finely chopped

- 1/2 bell pepper, finely chopped

- 1 bay leaf

- 1/2 teaspoon salt

- 1/4 teaspoon dried oregano, crumbled

- 2 yellow-fleshed potatoes

- 2 eggs, lightly beaten with 2 tablespoons water

- 15 medium dough circles

Cook the sausage in a skillet using oil for a few minutes. Drain the oil and place them in bowl. Using the same skillet add the onions and let them cook for 15 minutes. Add the garlic followed by bell pepper, the bay leaf, salt and finally the oregano and let them cook for 15 minutes.

Peel and cut the potato into ½ inch pieces. Add the potato pieces into the onion mixture and let them cook till the potatoes a little tender. Then add the mixture to the sausage and stir well, remember to remove the bay leaf and let the mixture cool.

The oven should be preheated to 400 degrees. Using a tablespoon put two spoonfuls of fillings on the center of the circle. Cover the edges of the dough with egg wash, then fold and seal the edges together. Place the dough on a baking pan and use egg wash on the top before baking in the oven for 25 minutes.

## BEEFY EGG EMPANADAS

- 1/2 lb ground beef

- 1/4 cup onion, finely chopped

- 2 tablespoons raisins, finely chopped

- 2 tablespoons chopped green olives

- 1/4 teaspoon salt

- 1/8 teaspoon pepper

- 1/4 cup cottage cheese

- 1 hardboiled egg, peeled and chopped

- 1 egg, separated

- 1 teaspoon water

- 15 small dough circles

- 2 teaspoons milk

Using a skillet cook the ground beef until it changes color to brown and drain. In the same skillet add the onions followed by olives, salt and pepper and let the mixture cook for 5 minutes.

Add the cottage cheese and the hard cooked egg.

The oven should be preheated to 400 degrees. Beat the egg white and add water, place it aside. Using a small tablespoon add one spoon of the beef mixture in the center of each circle and finish it off by brushing the edges with egg white.

Fold and seal the dough circles over the fillings. Place them on a baking pan. Prepare a mixture of egg yolk and milk and brush it on top of the dough circles. Bake them for 20 minutes

## CHEESY SAUSAGE AND EGG EMPANADAS

- 6 oz cream cheese, softened

- 1 1/2 tablespoons minced fresh parsley

- 3/4 teaspoon seasoned salt

- 1/4 teaspoon black pepper

- 2/3 cup shredded sharp cheddar cheese

- 2 tablespoons butter

- 5 large eggs, beaten

- 1/4 cup shredded cheddar cheese

- 1 can refrigerated jumbo flaky biscuits

- 1/2 lb sausage, cooked and crumbled

- 1 egg white, lightly beaten

You start by preheating the oven to 375 degrees. Get a large bowl and add the cream cheese, followed by the parsley, seasoned salt, pepper and finally the cheese and blend.

Using a skillet melt the butter. Add the eggs and wait till they are slightly thickened. Then remove the skillet from the stove and let the contents cool.

Level each biscuit into a large circle take the cream cheese mixture and spread it over the dough circles. On top of the dough finish with scrambled eggs and sausages.

Fold dough in half and seal off the edges. Place them on a baking sheet and use the egg white to finish off the top. Bake the dough in the oven for 16 minutes.

## EASY PIZZA EMPANADAS

- 1 can pizza sauce

- 2 cups shredded mozzarella cheese

- 1 1/2 cups sliced pepperoni

- 15 small dough circles

In the middle of each dough circle add one tablespoon of pizza sauce. Use the pepperoni and the cheese to finish off the top. Fold and seal off the edges of the dough. Then place them on a baking sheet and bake at 375 degrees for 12 minutes.

## CHEESEBURGER EMPANADAS

- 1 lb ground beef

- 1 garlic clove

- 1 teaspoon salt

- 1 (15 ounce) cans fresh cut corn, drained

- 1/2 cup chopped onion

- 8 ounces grated cheddar cheese

- 1 cup salsa

- 2 cans large refrigerated biscuits

Using a skillet cook the ground beef till it turns brown, add the salt and the pepper and let it to cool. Using a large bowl add the corn, followed by the cheese, salsa and mix. Then add the beef.

Flatten each biscuit, using a tablespoon put the filling in the middle of the dough. Fold and seal the edges off. Then place the dough on a baking pan and put it in the oven at 375 degrees for 12 minutes.

# EASY VEGETARIAN EMPANADAS

- 1 can re-fried beans

- 1 container fresh salsa

- 1 cup chopped mushrooms

- 1/2 cup diced red onion

- 1 pkg shredded vegan cheese

- 2 cans refrigerated biscuits

- Avocado

Start by preheating the oven to 400 degrees. Using a large bowl add and mix together the beans, salsa, mushrooms, and lastly the onions. Roll each biscuit flat. Using a table spoon put the filling in the middle of the dough and using the cheese to finish off the top. Fold and seal the dough off

Place the dough on the baking sheet and put it in the oven for 15 minutes. Serve with a slice of avocado.

# CHEESY PANCETTA EMPANADAS

- 15 medium dough circles

- 2 leeks, white and tender green parts only, sliced

- 10 oz thick pancetta, diced

- 2 cups grated Swiss cheese

- 1 cup raisins

- Dash of nutmeg

- Salt and pepper to taste

- 1 egg, beaten

Using a skillet cook the pancetta until crispy and drain it. Add the leeks and let the mixture cook for 10 minutes, then remove it from the stove and let it cool. In a large bowl add the cheese, followed by the raisins, nutmeg salt and finally the pepper. Then add the meat and leeks to the mixture and blend.

Using a table spoon put the filling in the middle of the dough. Fold and seal of the edges of the dough. Finish off the top with an egg mixture. The oven should be preheated to 400 degrees. Place the dough in the oven for 25 minutes.

## CHILI AND POTATO EMPANADAS

- 15 medium dough circles

- 1/2 cup left over mashed potatoes

- 1/4 cup chili pepper, roasted and peeled

- 1/4 cup grated pepper jack cheese

- 1/2 cup grated Cheddar cheese

- 1 egg and 1 tablespoon of water mixed together

Using a large bowl add the potatoes, pepper and cheese and mix. Using a tablespoon place the filling in the middle of the dough. Fold and seal off the edges and finish off the top with an egg mixture. Make sure that the oven is preheated to 400 degrees before place them in. let them bake for 25 minutes.

- 1 cup sofrito*

- 1 pkg frozen seafood mix, thawed and drained

- 1 tablespoon chopped cilantro

- 20 medium dough circles

Using a large bowl cook the sofrito then add the seafood mix stirring continually. After few minutes remove it from the stove and add the cilantro and let the mixture cool.

Using tablespoon, place the seafood mixture in the middle of the dough. Fold and seal off the edges. The oven should be preheated to 400 degrees before baking for 25 minutes.

*Sofrito Recipe:

2 green bell peppers, seeded and chopped

1 red bell peppers, seeded and chopped

10 chili peppers, seeded and chopped

3 medium tomatoes, chopped

4 onions cut into large chunks

3 garlic cloves, peeled

25 cilantro leaves with stems

1 tablespoon salt

1 tablespoon black pepper

Put are the ingredients in a blender and mix them until the mixture resembles a chunky salsa.

# CHEESY HAM EMPANADAS

- 15 small dough circles

- 1/2 lb smoked ham, finely chopped

- 1/2 lb feta cheese, crumbled

- 1/2 lb grated cheddar cheese

Using a large bowl add the ham, followed by the feta cheese, and cheddar cheese. Using a tablespoon place the mixture on the center of each dough circle. Fold and seal off the edges.

Put the pies on a baking pan and bake at 350 degrees for 12 minutes.

# CHEESY BLACK BEAN EMPANADAS

- 15 small dough circles

- 1 egg

- 1 tablespoon water

- 1/2 pound ground pork

- 1 small red pepper, diced

- 4 medium green onions, chopped

- 1 clove garlic, minced

- 1/2 cup tomato sauce

- 1 teaspoon ground cumin

- 1 teaspoon chili powder

- 1/8 teaspoon crushed red pepper

- 1 1/2 cups shredded Cheddar cheese

- 1 can black beans, rinsed and drained

- 1/4 cup chopped fresh cilantro leaves

Start by preheating the oven to 375 degrees. Using a large bowl beat the egg and add water and use the fork to stir.

Using a skillet, cook the pork until it changes color to brown. Add the cut red pepper, followed by the garlic and cook until it becomes tender. Then add the tomato sauce, cumin, chili powder and lastly the crushed red pepper. Reduce the heat and let the mixture cook for another 5 minutes.

After the 5 minutes are up remove it from the stove and add the cheese, beans and the cilantro. Leave the mixture to cool.

Using a tablespoon place the pork mixture on each of the dough circles and use water to brush off the edges. Then fold and seal off the edges of the dough. Place it on a baking pan and finish off the top with the egg mixture.

Bake the Empanadas for 15 minutes.

## THANK YOU

If you have truly found value in my publication please take a minute and rate my book, I'd be eternally grateful if you left a review. As an independent author I rely on reviews for my livelihood and it gives me great pleasure to see my work is appreciated.

Made in United States
Orlando, FL
19 December 2024